Handbook of Bears

Editor

Ricarda Whittaker

Scribbles

Year of Publication 2018

ISBN : 9789352979820

Book Published by

Scribbles

(An Imprint of Alpha Editions)

email - alphaedis@gmail.com

Produced by: PediaPress GmbH

Limburg an der Lahn

Germany

http://pediapress.com/

Contents

Bear

<indicator name="pp-default"> 🔒 </indicator> <indicator name="good-star"> ⊕ </indicator>

Bears	
Temporal range: 38–0 Ma	
PreЄЄ OSD C P T J K PgN	
Late Eocene – Recent	
Brown Bear in Alaska	
Scientific classification 🖉	
Kingdom:	Animalia
Phylum:	Chordata
Class:	Mammalia
Order:	Carnivora
Infraorder:	Arctoidea
Family:	**Ursidae** G. Fischer de Waldheim, 1817
Subfamilies	
† Amphicynodontinae † Hemicyoninae † Ursavinae † Agriotheriinae Ailuropodinae Tremarctinae Ursinae	

Bears are carnivoran mammals of the family **Ursidae**. They are classified as caniforms, or doglike carnivorans. Although only eight species of bears are extant, they are widespread, appearing in a wide variety of habitats throughout the Northern Hemisphere and partially in the Southern Hemisphere. Bears are found on the continents of North America, South America, Europe, and Asia.

Common characteristics of modern bears include large bodies with stocky legs, long snouts, small rounded ears, shaggy hair, plantigrade paws with five non-retractile claws, and short tails.

While the polar bear is mostly carnivorous, and the giant panda feeds almost entirely on bamboo, the remaining six species are omnivorous with varied diets. With the exception of courting individuals and mothers with their young, bears are typically solitary animals. They may be diurnal or nocturnal and have an excellent sense of smell. Despite their heavy build and awkward gait, they are adept runners, climbers, and swimmers. Bears use shelters, such as caves and logs, as their dens; most species occupy their dens during the winter for a long period of hibernation, up to 100 days.

Bears have been hunted since prehistoric times for their meat and fur; they have been used for bear-baiting and other forms of entertainment, such as being made to dance. With their powerful physical presence, they play a prominent role in the arts, mythology, and other cultural aspects of various human societies. In modern times, bears have come under pressure through encroachment on their habitats and illegal trade in bear parts, including the Asian bile bear market. The IUCN lists six bear species as vulnerable or endangered, and even least concern species, such as the brown bear, are at risk of extirpation in certain countries. The poaching and international trade of these most threatened populations are prohibited, but still ongoing.

Etymology

The English word "bear" comes from Old English *bera* and belongs to a family of names for the bear in Germanic languages, such as Swedish *björn*, also used as a first name, that originate from an adjective meaning "brown". "Bear" therefore originally meant "the brown one." This terminology for the animal originated as a taboo avoidance term: proto-Germanic tribes replaced their original word for bear – *arkto* – with this euphemistic expression out of fear that speaking the animal's true name might cause it to appear.

Bear taxon names such as Arctoidea and *Helarctos* come from the ancient Greek word ἄρκτος (*arktos*), meaning bear, as do the names "arctic" and "antarctic", from the constellation Ursa Major, the "Great Bear", prominent in the northern sky.

Bear taxon names such as Ursidae and *Ursus* come from Latin *Ursus/Ursa*, he-bear/she-bear. The female first name "Ursula", originally derived from a Christian saint's name, means "little she-bear" (diminutive of Latin *ursa*). In Switzerland, the male first name "Urs" is especially popular, while the name of the canton and city of Bern is derived from *Bär*, German for bear. The

Germanic name Bernard (including Bernhardt and similar forms) means "bear-brave", "bear-hardy", or "bold bear". The Old English name Beowulf is a kenning, "bee-wolf", for bear, in turn meaning a brave warrior.[1]

Taxonomy and phylogeny

The family Ursidae is one of nine families in the suborder Caniformia, or "doglike" carnivorans, within the order Carnivora. Bears' closest living relatives are the pinnipeds, canids, and musteloids. Modern bears comprise eight species in three subfamilies: Ailuropodinae (monotypic with the giant panda), Tremarctinae (monotypic with the spectacled bear), and Ursinae (containing six species divided into one to three genera, depending on the authority). Nuclear chromosome analysis show that the karyotype of the six ursine bears is nearly identical, with each having 74 chromosomes, whereas the giant panda has 42 chromosomes and the spectacled bear 52. These smaller numbers can be explained by the fusing of some chromosomes, and the banding patterns on these match those of the ursine species, but differ from those of procyonids, which supports the inclusion of these two species in Ursidae rather than in Procyonidae, where they had been placed by some earlier authorities.

Evolution

The earliest members of Ursidae belong to the extinct subfamily Amphicynodontinae, including *Parictis* (late Eocene to early middle Miocene, 38–18 Mya) and the slightly younger *Allocyon* (early Oligocene, 34–30 Mya), both from North America. These animals looked very different from today's bears, being small and raccoon-like in overall appearance, with diets perhaps more similar to that of a badger. *Parictis* does not appear in Eurasia and Africa until the Miocene. It is unclear whether late-Eocene ursids were also present in Eurasia, although faunal exchange across the Bering land bridge may have been possible during a major sea level low stand as early as the late Eocene (about 37 Mya) and continuing into the early Oligocene. European genera morphologically very similar to *Allocyon*, and to the much younger American *Kolponomos* (about 18 Mya), are known from the Oligocene, including *Amphicticeps* and *Amphicynodon*. There has been various morphological evidence linking amphicynodontines with pinnipeds, as both groups were semi-aquatic, otter-like mammals. In addition to the support of the pinniped–amphicynodontine clade, other morphological and some molecular evidence supports bears being the closet living relatives to pinnipeds.

The raccoon-sized, dog-like *Cephalogale* is the oldest-known member of the subfamily Hemicyoninae, which first appeared during the middle Oligocene in

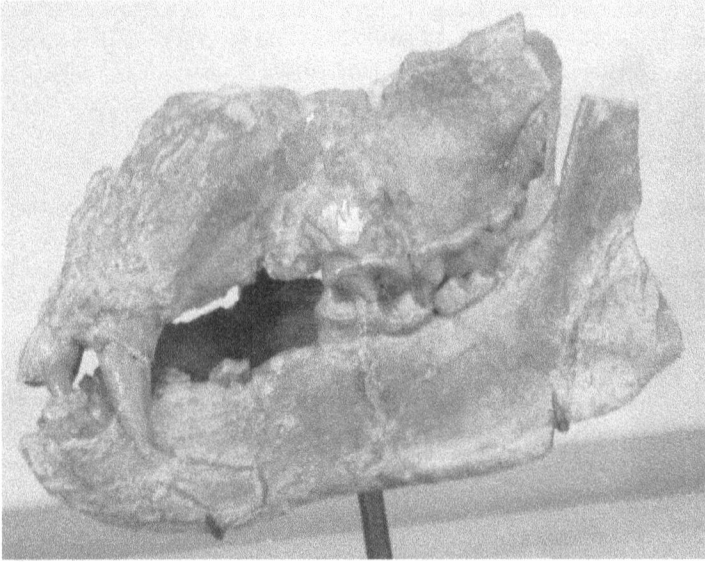

Figure 1: *Plithocyon armagnacensis skull, a member of
the extinct subfamily Hemicyoninae from the Miocene*

Eurasia about 30 Mya. The subfamily includes the younger genera *Phobero-cyon* (20–15 Mya), and *Plithocyon* (15–7 Mya). A *Cephalogale*-like species
gave rise to the genus *Ursavus* during the early Oligocene (30–28 Mya); this
genus proliferated into many species in Asia and is ancestral to all living bears.
Species of *Ursavus* subsequently entered North America, together with *Amph-icynodon* and *Cephalogale*, during the early Miocene (21–18 Mya). Members
of the living lineages of bears diverged from *Ursavus* between 15 and 20 Mya,
likely via the species *Ursavus elmensis*. Based on genetic and morphological
data, the Ailuropodinae (pandas) were the first to diverge from other living
bears about 19 Mya, although no fossils of this group have been found before
about 5 Mya.

The New World short-faced bears (Tremarctinae) differentiated from Ursinae
following a dispersal event into North America during the mid-Miocene (about
13 Mya). They invaded South America ($\approx$1 Ma) following formation of the
Isthmus of Panama. Their earliest fossil representative is *Plionarctos* in North
America ($\sim$ 10–2 Ma). This genus is probably the direct ancestor to the North
American short-faced bears (genus *Arctodus*), the South American short-faced
bears (*Arctotherium*), and the spectacled bears, *Tremarctos*, represented by
both an extinct North American species (*T. floridanus*), and the lone surviving

Figure 2: *Fossil of the cave bear (Ursus spelaeus), a relative of the brown bear and polar bear from the Pleistocene epoch in Europe*

representative of the Tremarctinae, the South American spectacled bear (*T. ornatus*).

The subfamily Ursinae experienced a dramatic proliferation of taxa about 5.3–4.5 Mya, coincident with major environmental changes; the first members of the genus *Ursus* appeared around this time. The sloth bear is a modern survivor of one of the earliest lineages to diverge during this radiation event (5.3 Mya); it took on its peculiar morphology, related to its diet of termites and ants, no later than by the early Pleistocene. By 3–4 Mya, the species *Ursus minimus* appears in the fossil record of Europe; apart from its size, it was nearly identical to today's Asian black bear. It is likely ancestral to all bears within Ursinae, perhaps aside from the sloth bear. Two lineages evolved from *U. minimus*: the black bears (including the sun bear, the Asian black bear, and the American black bear); and the brown bears (which includes the polar bear). Modern brown bears evolved from *U. minimus* via *Ursus etruscus*, which itself is ancestral to the extinct Pleistocene cave bear. Species of Ursinae have migrated repeatedly into North America from Eurasia as early as 4 Mya during the early Pliocene.[2] The polar bear is the most recently evolved species and descended from the brown bear around 400,000 years ago.

Phylogeny

The bears form a clade within the Carnivora. The red panda is not a bear but a musteloid. The cladogram is based on molecular phylogeny of six genes in Flynn, 2005. <templatestyles src="Clade/styles.css"></templatestyles>

Car-   <templatestyles src="Clade/styles.css"></templatestyles>
nivora

        Feliformia

      Cani-   <templatestyles src="Clade/styles.css"></templatestyles>
      formia

             Canidae

             Arc-   <templatestyles src="Clade/styles.css"></templatestyles>
             toidea   <templatestyles src="Clade/styles.css"></templatestyles>

               † Hemicyonidae

              Ursidae

               <templatestyles src="Clade/styles.css"></templatestyles>

                Pinnipedia

             Musteloidea   <templatestyles src="Clade/styles.css"></templatestyles>

                Ailuridae, inc. red panda

                Other musteloids

There are two phylogenetic hypotheses on the relationships among extant and fossil bear spcies. One is all species of bears are classified in seven subfamilies as adopted here and related articles: Amphicynodontinae, Hemicyoninae, Ursavinae, Agriotheriinae, Ailuropodinae, Tremarctinae, and Ursinae. Below is a cladogram of the subfamilies of bears after McLellan and Reiner (1992) and Qiu et a. (2014): <templatestyles src="Clade/styles.css"></templatestyles>

Ur-   <templatestyles src="Clade/styles.css"></templatestyles>
si-
dae

† Amphicynodontinae

<templatestyles src="Clade/styles.css"></templatestyles>
† Hemicyoninae

<templatestyles src="Clade/styles.css"></templatestyles>
† Ursavinae

<templatestyles src="Clade/styles.css"></templatestyles>
† Agriotheriinae

<templatestyles src="Clade/styles.css"></templatestyles>
Ailuropodinae

<templatestyles src="Clade/styles.css"></templatestyles>
Tremarctinae

Ursinae

The second alternative phylogenetic hypothesis was implemented by McKenna et al. (1997) is to classify all the bear species into the superfamily **Ursoidea**, with Hemicyoninae and Agriotheriinae being classified in the family "Hemicyonidae". Amphicynodontinae under this classification were classified as stem-pinnipeds in the superfamily Phocoidea. In the McKenna and Bell classification both bears and pinnipeds in a parvorder of carnivoran mammals known as Ursida, along with the extinct bear dogs of the family Amphicyonidae. Below is the cladogram based on McKenna and Bell (1997) classification: <templatestyles src="Clade/styles.css"></templatestyles>

Ursida

<templatestyles src="Clade/styles.css"></templatestyles>

<templatestyles src="Clade/styles.css"></templatestyles>

† Amphicyonidae

<templatestyles src="Clade/styles.css"></templatestyles>
<templatestyles src="Clade/styles.css"></templatestyles>

Pho-   <templatestyles src="Clade/styles.css"></templatestyles>
coidea   † Amphicynodontidae

        Pinnipedia

<templatestyles src="Clade/styles.css"></templatestyles>

Ursoidea

<templatestyles src="Clade/styles.css"></templatestyles>

  <templatestyles src="Clade/styles.css"></templatestyles>
    † Hemicyonidae   <templatestyles src="Clade/styles.css"></templatestyles>
                      † Hemicyoninae

                    † Agriotheriinae

  <templatestyles src="Clade/styles.css"></templatestyles>
  Ursi- <templatestyles src="Clade/styles.css"></templatestyles>
  dae   † Ursavinae

          <templatestyles src="Clade/styles.css"></templatestyles>
            <templatestyles src="Clade/styles.css"></templatestyles>
            Ailuropodinae

          <templatestyles src="Clade/styles.css"></templatestyles>
            <templatestyles src="Clade/styles.css"></templatestyles>
            Tremarctinae

            Ursinae

The phylogeny of extant bear species is shown in a cladogram based on complete mitochondrial DNA sequences from Yu et al., 2007. The giant panda, followed by the spectacled bear are clearly the oldest species. The relationships of the other species are not very well resolved, though the polar bear and the brown bear form a close grouping.

<templatestyles src="Clade/styles.css"></templatestyles>

Ur-si-dae <templatestyles src="Clade/styles.css"></templatestyles>

<templatestyles src="Clade/styles.css"></templatestyles>
<templatestyles src="Clade/styles.css"></templatestyles>
<templatestyles src="Clade/styles.css"></templatestyles>
<templatestyles src="Clade/styles.css"></templatestyles>

Brown bear

Polar bear

<templatestyles src="Clade/styles.css"></templatestyles>
<templatestyles src="Clade/styles.css"></templatestyles>

Asian black bear

American black bear

Sun bear

Sloth bear

Spectacled bear

Giant panda

Classification

- **Family Ursidae** (G. Fischer de Waldheim, 1817)
  - Subfamily † Amphicynodontinae (Simpson, 1945)
    - † *Amphicticeps* (Matthew and Granger, 1924)
      - † *Amphicticeps makhchinus* (Wang et al., 2005)

Figure 3: *Restoration of Kolponomos a large marine bear*

Figure 4: *Restoration of Hemicyon by Jay Matternes*

Figure 5: *Mandible of Agriotherium. This genus that existed from the Miocene to the Pleistocene is the only known ursid to have lived in sub-Saharan Africa.*

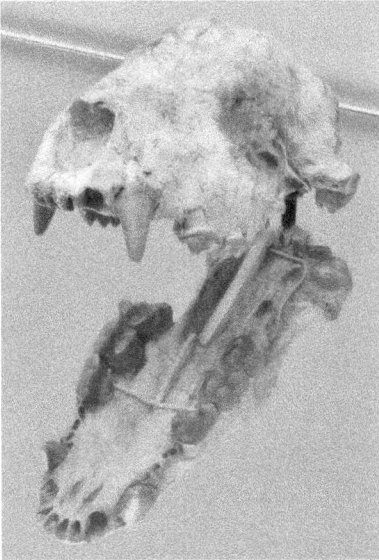

Figure 6: *Skull of Indarctos atticus. Indarctos was a Miocene genus found across the northern hemisphere.*

Figure 7: *Giant panda (Ailuropoda melanoleuca) eating bamboo leaves*

Figure 8: *Restoration of Arctotherium, a South American Pleistocene genus from a lineage whose only survivor is the spectacled bear. It is the largest bear ever found and contender for the largest carnivorous land mammal known.*

Figure 9: *A sun bear (Helarctos malayanus) sitting upright*

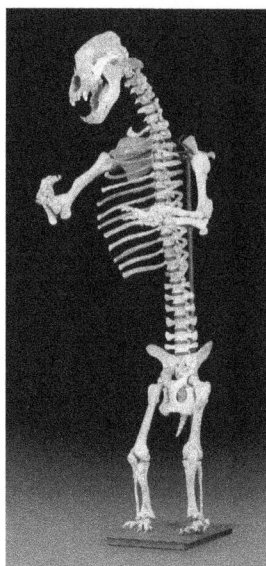

Figure 10: *Ice age cave bear (Ursus spelaeus) from 150,000 BCE*

Figure 11: *A brown bear (Ursus arctos) surveying the landscape*

- † *Amphicticeps dorog* (Wang et al., 2005)
- † *Amphicticeps shackelfordi* (Matthew and Granger, 1924)
- † *Parictis* (Scott, 1893)
  - † *Parictis primaevus* (Scott, 1893)
  - † *Parictis personi* (Chaffee, 1954)
  - † *Parictis montanus* (Clark & Guensburg, 1972)
  - † *Parictis parvus* (Clark & Beerbower, 1967)
  - † *Parictis gilpini* (Clark & Guensburg, 1972)
  - † *Parictis dakotensis* (Clark, 1936)
- † *Kolponomos* (Stirton, 1960)
  - † *Kolponomos newportensis* (Tedford et al., 1994)
  - † *Kolponomos clallamensis* (Stirton, 1960)
- † *Allocyon* (Merriam, 1930)
  - † *Allocyon loganensis* (Merriam, 1930)
- † *Pachycynodon* (Schlosser, 1888)
  - † *Pachycynodon tedfordi* (Wang & Qiu, 2003)
  - † *Pachycynodon tenuis* (Teilhard de Chardin, 1915)
  - † *Pachycynodon filholi* (Schlosser, 1888)
  - † *Pachycynodon boriei* (Filhol, 1876)
  - † *Pachycynodon crassirostris* (Schlosser, 1888)
- † *Amphicynodon* (Filhol, 1881)

- † *Amphicynodon mongoliensis* (Janovskaja, 1970)
- † *Amphicynodon teilhardi* (Matthew and Granger, 1924)
- † *Amphicynodon typicus* (Schlosser, 1888)
- † *Amphicynodon chardini* (Cirot and De Bonis, 1992)
- † *Amphicynodon cephalogalinus* (Teilhard, 1915)
- † *Amphicynodon gracilis* (Filhol, 1874)
- † *Amphicynodon crassirostris* (Filhol, 1876)
- † *Amphicynodon brachyrostris* (Filhol, 1876)
- † *Amphicynodon leptorhynchus* (Filhol, 1874)
- † *Amphicynodon velaunus* (Aymard, 1846)
- Subfamily † Hemicyoninae (Frick, 1926)
  - Tribe † Cephalogalini (de Bonis, 2013)
    - † *Adelpharctos* (de Bonis, 1971)
      - † *Adelpharctos ginsburgi* (de Bonis, 2011)
      - † *Adelpharctos mirus* (de Bonis, 1971)
    - † *Cyonarctos* (de Bonis, 2013)
      - † *Cyonarctos dessei* (de Bonis, 2013)
    - † *Phoberogale* (Ginsburg & Morales, 1995)
      - † *Phoberogale minor* (Filhol, 1877)
      - † *Phoberogale bonali* (Helbing, 1928)
      - † *Phoberogale depereti* (Viret, 1929)
      - † *Phoberogale gracile* (Pomel, 1847)
    - † *Filholictis* (de Bonis, 2013)
      - † *Filholictis filholi* (Munier-Chalmas, 1877)
    - † *Cephalogale* (Jourdan, 1862)
      - † *Cephalogale shareri* (Wang, et al., 2009)
      - † *Cephalogale gergoviensis* (Viret, 1929)
      - † *Cephalogale ginesticus* (Kuss, 1962)
      - † *Cephalogale geoffroyi* (Jourdan, 1862)
  - Tribe † Phoberocyonini (Ginsburg & Morales, 1995)
    - † *Plithocyon* (Ginsburg, 1955)
      - † *Plithocyon armagnacensis* (Ginsburg, 1955)
      - † *Plithocyon statzlingii* (Frick, 1926)
      - † *Plithocyon bruneti* (Ginsburg, 1980)
      - † *Plithocyon barstowensis* (Frick, 1926)
      - † *Plithocyon ursinus* (Cope, 1875)
    - † *Phoberocyon* (Ginsburg, 1955)
      - † *Phoberocyon hispanicus* (Ginsburg & Morales, 1998)
      - † *Phoberocyon dehmi* (Ginsburg, 1955)
      - † *Phoberocyon huerzeleri* (Ginsburg, 1955)
      - † *Phoberocyon aurelianensis* (Mayet, 1908)
      - † *Phoberocyon youngi* (Xiang et al., 1986)

- • † *Phoberocyon johnhenryi* (White, 1947)
- • Tribe † Hemicyonini (Frick, 1926)
  - • † *Zaragocyon* (Ginsburg & Morales, 1995)
    - • † *Zaragocyon daamsi* (Ginsburg & Morales, 1995)
  - • † *Dinocyon* (Jourdan, 1861)
    - • † *Dinocyon aurelianensis* (Frick, 1926)
    - • † *Dinocyon sansaniensis* (Frick, 1926)
    - • † *Dinocyon thenardi* (Jourdan, 1861)
  - • † *Hemicyon* (Lartet, 1851)
    - • † *Hemicyon barbouri* (Colbert, 1941)
    - • † *Hemicyon teilhardi* (Colbert, 1939)
    - • † *Hemicyon grivensis* (Frick, 1926)
    - • † *Hemicyon minor* (Dépéret, 1887)
    - • † *Hemicyon sansaniensis* (Lartet, 1851)
- • Subfamily † Ursavinae (Hendey, 1980)
  - • † *Ballusia* (Ginsburg & Morales, 1998)
    - • † *Ballusia elmensis* (Stehlin, 1917)
    - • † *Ballusia hareni* (Ginsburg, 1989)
    - • † *Ballusia orientalis* (Qiu et al., 1985)
  - • † *Ursavus* (Schlosser, 1899)
    - • † *Ursavus brevirhinus* (Hofmann, 1887)
    - • † *Ursavus primaevus* (Gaillard, 1899)
    - • † *Ursavus intermedius* (Koenigswald, 1925)
    - • † *Ursavus pawniensis* (Frick, 1926)
    - • † *Ursavus ehrenbergi* (Brunner, 1942)
    - • † *Ursavus sylvestris* (Qiu & Qi, 1990)
    - • † *Ursavus isorei* (Ginsburg & Morales, 1998)
    - • † *Ursavus tedfordi* (Zhanxiang et al., 2014)
- • Subfamily † Agrotheriinae (Kretzoi, 1929)
  - • † *Agriotherium* (Wagner, 1837)
    - • † *Agriotherium myanmarensis* (Ogino et al., 2011)
    - • † *Agriotherium insigne* (Gervais, 1859)
    - • † *Agriotherium inexpetans* (Qiu et al., 1991)
    - • † *Agriotherium palaeindicus* (Lydekker, 1878)
    - • † *Agriotherium sivalensis* (Falconer & Cautley, 1836)
    - • † *Agriotherium africanum* (Hendey, 1972)
    - • † *Agriotherium coffeyi* (Dalquest, 1986)
    - • † *Agriotherium gregoryi* (Frick, 1926)
    - • † *Agriotherium schneideri* (Sellards, 1916)
- • Subfamily Ailuropodinae (Grevé, 1894)
  - • Tribe † Indarctini (Abella et al., 2012)
    - • † *Miomaci* (de Bonis et al., 2017)

- † *Miomaci pannonicum* (de Bonis et al., 2017)
- † *Indarctos* (Pilgrim, 1913)
  - † *Indarctos punjabensis* (Lydekker, 1884)
  - † *Indarctos zdanskyi* (Qiu & Tedford, 2003)
  - † *Indarctos sinensis* (Zdansky, 1924)
  - † *Indarctos vireti* (Villalta & Crusafont, 1943)
  - † *Indarctos arctoides* (Deperet, 1895)
  - † *Indarctos anthracitis* (Weithofer, 1888)
  - † *Indarctos salmontanus* (Pilgrim, 1913)
  - † *Indarctos atticus* (Weithofer, 1888)
  - † *Indarctos bakalovi* (Kovachev, 1988)
  - † *Indarctos lagrelli* (Zdansky, 1924)
  - † *Indarctos oregonensis* (Merriam et al., 1916)
  - † *Indarctos nevadensis* (Macdonald, 1959)
- Tribe Ailuropodini (Grevé, 1894)
  - † *Kretzoiarctos* (Abella et al., 2012)
    - † *Kretzoiarctos beatrix* (Abella et al., 2011)
  - † *Agriarctos* (Kretzoi, 1942)
    - † *Agriarctos depereti* (Schlosser, 1902)
    - † *Agriarctos vighi* (Kretzoi, 1942)
    - † *Agriarctos gaali* (Kretzoi, 1942)
  - † *Ailurarctos* (Qi et al., 1989)
    - † *Ailurarctos yuanmouensis* (Zong, 1997)
    - † *Ailurarctos lufengensis* (Qi et al., 1989)
  - *Ailuropoda* (Milne-Edwards, 1870)
    - † *Ailuropoda microta* (Pei, 1962)
    - † *Ailuropoda wulingshanensis* (Wang & Alii, 1982)
    - † *Ailuropoda minor* (Pei, 1962)
    - † *Ailuropoda baconi* (Woodward 1915)
    - *Ailuropoda melanoleuca* (David, 1869) – Giant panda
- Subfamily Tremarctinae (Merriam & Stock, 1925)
  - † *Plionarctos* (Frick, 1926)
    - † *Plionarctos harroldorum* (Tedford & Martin, 2001)
    - † *Plionarctos edensis* (Frick, 1926)
  - † *Arctodus* (Leidy, 1854)
    - † *Arctodus simus* (Cope, 1879)
    - † *Arctodus pristinus* (Leidy, 1854)
  - † *Arctotherium* (Burmeister, 1879)
    - † *Arctotherium angustidens* (Gervais & Ameghino, 1880)
    - † *Arctotherium vetustum* (Ameghino, 1885)
    - † *Arctotherium wingei* (Ameghino, 1902)
    - † *Arctotherium bonariense* (Gervais, 1852)

- † *Arctotherium tarijense* (Ameghino, 1902)
- *Tremarctos* (Gervais, 1855)
  - † *Tremarctos floridanus* (Gildey, 1928)
  - *Tremarctos ornatus* (Cuvier, 1825) – spectacled bear
- Subfamily Ursinae (G. Fischer de Waldheim, 1817)
  - *Ursus* (Linnaeus, 1758)
    - † *Ursus boeckhi* (Schlosser, 1899)
    - † *Ursus abstrusus* (Bjork, 1970)
    - † *Ursus yinanensis* (Li, 1993)
    - † *Ursus ruscinensis* (Depéret, 1890)
    - † *Ursus theobaldi* (Lydekker, 1884)
  - *Ursus ursinus* (Shaw, 1791) – sloth bear
  - † *Ursus sinomalayanus* (Thenius, 1947)
  - *Ursus malayanus* (Raffles, 1821) – sun bear
  - † *Ursus pyrenaicus* (Depéret, 1892)
  - † *Ursus minimus* (Devèze & Bouillet, 1827)
  - *Ursus thibetanus* (G. Cuvier, 1823) – Asiatic black bear
  - *Ursus americanus* (Pallas, 1780) – American black bear
  - † *Ursus etruscus* (Cuvier, 1823)
  - † *Ursus dolinensis* (Garcia & Arsuaga, 2001)
  - † *Ursus savini* (Andrews, 1922)
  - † *Ursus deningeri* (Richenau, 1904)
  - † *Ursus kudarensis* (Baryshnikov, 1985)
  - † *Ursus rossicus* (Borissiak, 1930)
  - † *Ursus ingressus* (Rabeder, Hofreiter, Nagel & Withalm 2004)
  - † *Ursus deningeri* (Richenau, 1904)
  - † *Ursus spelaeus* (Rosenmüller, 1794)
  - *Ursus maritimus* (Phipps, 1774) – polar bear
  - *Ursus arctos* (Linnaeus, 1758) – brown bear

Physical characteristics

Size

<templatestyles src="Multiple_image/styles.css" />

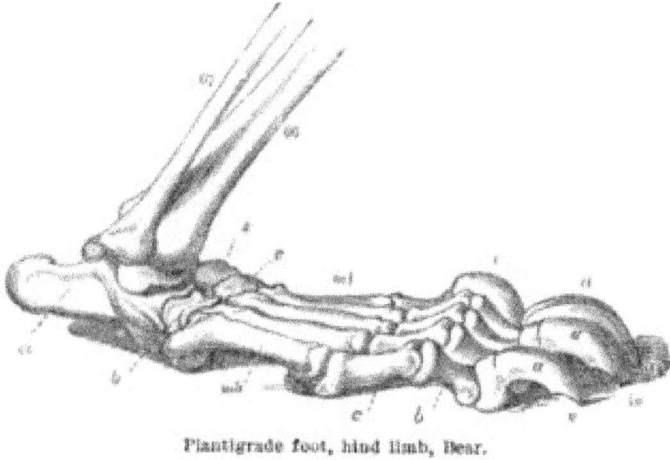

Plantigrade foot, hind limb, Bear.

Figure 12: *Unlike most other Carnivora, bears have plantigrade feet. Drawing by Richard Owen, 1866.*

Polar bear (left) and sun bear, the largest and smallest species respectively, on average

The bear family includes the most massive extant terrestrial members of the order Carnivora.[3] as marine mammals</ref> The polar bear is considered to be the largest extant species,[4] with adult males weighing 350–700 kg (772–1,543 lb) and measuring 2.4–3 metres (7 ft 10 in–9 ft 10 in) in total length. The smallest species is the sun bear, which ranges 25–65 kg (55–143 lb) in weight and 100–140 cm (39–55 in) in length. Prehistoric North and South American short-faced bears were the largest species known to have lived. The latter estimated to have weighed 1,600 kg (3,500 lb) and stood 3.4 m (11 ft) tall.[5] Body weight varies throughout the year in bears of temperate and arctic climates, as they build up fat reserves in the summer and autumn and lose weight during the winter.

Morphology

Bears are generally bulky and robust animals with short tails. They are sexually dimorphic with regard to size, with males typically being larger. Larger species

Figure 13: *Despite being quadrupeds, bears can stand and sit as humans do.*

tend to show increased levels of sexual dimorphism in comparison to smaller species. Relying as they do on strength rather than speed, bears have relatively short limbs with thick bones to support their bulk. The shoulder blades and the pelvis are correspondingly massive. The limbs are much straighter than those of the big cats as there is no need for them to flex in the same way due to the differences in their gait. The strong forelimbs are used to catch prey, to excavate dens, to dig out burrowing animals, to turn over rocks and logs to locate prey, and to club large creatures.

Unlike most other land carnivorans, bears are plantigrade. They distribute their weight toward the hind feet, which makes them look lumbering when they walk. They are capable of bursts of speed but soon tire, and as a result mostly rely on ambush rather than the chase. Bears can stand on their hind feet and sit up straight with remarkable balance. Their front paws are flexible enough to grasp fruit and leaves. Bears' non-retractable claws are used for digging, climbing, tearing, and catching prey. The claws on the front feet are larger than those on the back and may be a hindrance when climbing trees; black bears are the most arboreal of the bears, and have the shortest claws. Pandas are unique in having a bony extension on the wrist of the front feet which acts as a thumb, and is used for gripping bamboo shoots as the animals feed.

Most mammals have agouti hair, with each individual hair shaft having bands of colour corresponding to two different types of melanin pigment. Bears however

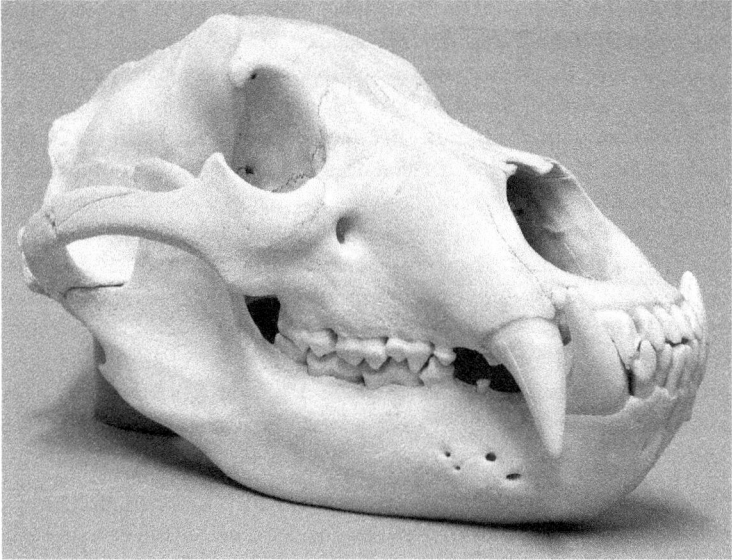

Figure 14: *Brown bear skull*

have a single type of melanin and the hairs have a single colour throughout their length, apart from the tip which is sometimes a different shade. The coat consists of long guard hairs, which form a protective shaggy covering, and short dense hairs which form an insulating layer trapping air close to the skin. The shaggy coat helps maintain body heat during winter hibernation and is shed in the spring leaving a shorter summer coat. Polar bears have hollow, translucent guard hairs which gain heat from the sun and conduct it to the dark-coloured skin below. They have a thick layer of blubber for extra insulation, and the soles of their feet have a dense pad of fur. Other than the bold black-and-white pelage of the panda, bears tend to be uniform in colour, although some species may have markings on the chest or face.

Bears have small rounded ears so as to minimise heat loss, but neither their hearing or sight are particularly acute. Unlike many other carnivorans they have colour vision, perhaps to help them distinguish ripe nuts and fruits. They are unique among carnivorans in not having touch-sensitive whiskers on the muzzle; however, they have an excellent sense of smell, better than that of the dog, or possibly any other mammal. They use smell for signalling to each other (either to warn off rivals or detect mates) and for finding food. Smell is the principal sense used by bears to locate most of their food, and they have excellent memories which helps them to relocate places where they have found food before.

The skulls of bears are massive, providing anchorage for the powerful mas-seter and temporal jaw muscles. The canine teeth are large but mostly used for display, and the molar teeth flat and crushing. Unlike most other mem-bers of the Carnivora, bears have relatively undeveloped carnassial teeth, and their teeth are adapted for a diet that includes a significant amount of veg-etable matter. Considerable variation occurs in dental formula even within a given species. This may indicate bears are still in the process of evolving from a mainly meat-eating diet to a predominantly herbivorous one. Polar bears ap-pear to have secondarily re-evolved carnassial-like cheek teeth, as their diets have switched back towards carnivory. Sloth bears lack lower central incisors and use their protusible lips for sucking up the termites on which they feed. The general dental formula for living bears is: 3.1.2–4.23.1.2–4.3. The struc-ture of the larynx of bears appears to be the most basal of the caniforms. They possess air pouches connected to the pharynx which may amplify their vocal-isations.

Bears have a fairly simple digestive system typical for carnivorans, with a single stomach, short undifferentiated intestines and no cecum. Even the herbivorous giant panda still has the digestive system of a carnivore, as well as carnivore-specific genes. Its ability to digest cellulose is ascribed to the microbes in its gut. Bears must spend much of their time feeding in order to gain enough nutrition from foliage. The panda, in particular, spends 12–15 hours a day feeding.

Distribution and habitat

Extant bears are found in sixty countries primarily in the Northern Hemisphere and are concentrated in Asia, North America, and Europe. An exception is the spectacled bear; native to South America, it inhabits the Andean region. The sun bear's range extends below the equator in Southeast Asia.[6] The Atlas bear, a subspecies of the brown bear was distributed in North Africa from Morocco to Libya, but it became extinct around the 1870s.

The most widespread species is the brown bear, which occurs from Western Europe eastwards through Asia to the western areas of North America. The American black bear is restricted to North America, and the polar bear is re-stricted to the Arctic Sea. All the remaining species of bear are Asian. They occur in a range of habitats which include tropical lowland rainforest, both coniferous and broadleaf forests, prairies, steppes, montane grassland, alpine scree slopes, Arctic tundra and in the case of the polar bear, ice floes. Bears may dig their dens in hillsides or use caves, hollow logs and dense vegetation for shelter.

Figure 15: *The spectacled bear is the only species found in South America.*

Behaviour and life history

Brown and American black bears are generally diurnal, meaning that they are active for the most part during the day, though they may forage substantially by night. Other species may be nocturnal, active at night, though female sloth bears with cubs may feed more at daytime to avoid competition from con-specifics and nocturnal predators.[7] Bears are overwhelmingly solitary and are considered to be the most asocial of all the Carnivora. The only times bears are encountered in small groups are mothers with young or occasional seasonal bounties of rich food (such as salmon runs). Fights between males can occur and older individuals may have extensive scarring, which suggests that maintaining dominance can be intense.[8] With their acute sense of smell, bears can locate carcasses from several kilometres away. They use olfaction to locate other foods, encounter mates, avoid rivals and recognise their cubs.

Feeding

Most bears are opportunistic omnivores and consume more plant than animal matter. They eat anything from leaves, roots, and berries to insects, carrion, fresh meat, and fish, and have digestive systems and teeth adapted to such a diet. At the extremes are the almost entirely herbivorous giant panda and the mostly carnivorous polar bear. However, all bears feed on any food source

Figure 16: *American black bear tracks at Superior National Forest, Minnesota, the United States of America*

Figure 17: *Giant panda feeding on bamboo at Smithsonian National Zoological Park, Washington, D. C. This species is almost entirely herbivorous.*

Figure 18: *Brown bear feeding on infrequent,*
but predictable, salmon migrations in Alaska

that becomes seasonally available.[9] For example, Asiatic black bears in Taiwan consume large numbers of acorns when these are most common, and switch to ungulates at other times of the year.

When foraging for plants, bears choose to eat them at the stage when they are at their most nutritious and digestible, typically avoiding older grasses, sedges and leaves. Hence, in more northern temperate areas, browsing and grazing is more common early in spring and later becomes more restricted. Knowing when plants are ripe for eating is a learned behaviour. Berries may be foraged in bushes or at the tops of trees, and bears try to maximize the number of berries consumed versus foliage. In autumn, some bear species forage large amounts of naturally fermented fruits, which affects their behaviour. Smaller bears climb trees to obtain mast (edible reproductive parts, such as acorns). Such masts can be very important to the diets of these species, and mast failures may result in long-range movements by bears looking for alternative food sources. Brown bears, with their powerful digging abilities, commonly eat roots. The panda's diet is over 99% bamboo, of 30 different species. Its strong jaws are adapted for crushing the tough stems of these plants, though they prefer to eat the more nutritious leaves.[10] Bromeliads can make up to 50% of the diet of the spectacled bear, which also has strong jaws to bite them open.[11]

Figure 19: *Polar bear feeding on a seal on an ice floe north of Svalbard, Norway. It is the most carnivorous species.*

The sloth bear, though not as specialised as polar bears and the panda, has lost several front teeth usually seen in bears, and developed a long, suctioning tongue to feed on the ants, termites, and other burrowing insects they favour. At certain times of the year, these insects can make up 90% of their diets. Some species may raid the nests of wasps and bees for the honey and immature insects, in spite of stinging from the adults. Sun bears use their long tongues to lick up both insects and honey.[12] Fish are an important source of food for some species, and brown bears in particular gather in large numbers at salmon runs. Typically, a bear plunges into the water and seizes a fish with its jaws or front paws. The preferred parts to eat are the brain and eggs. Small burrowing mammals like rodents may be dug out and eaten.

The brown bear and both species of black bears sometimes take large ungulates, such as deer and bovids, mostly the young and weak.[13] These animals may be taken by a short rush and ambush, though hiding young may be stiffed out and pounced on. The polar bear mainly preys on seals, stalking them from the ice or breaking into their dens. They primarily eat the highly digestible blubber.[14] Large mammalian prey is typically killed by a bite to the head or neck, or (in the case of young) simply pinned down and mauled. Predatory behaviour in bears is typically taught to the young by the mother.

Bears are prolific scavengers and kleptoparasites, stealing food caches from rodents, and carcasses from other predators. For hibernating species, weight gain is important as it provides nourishment during winter dormancy. A brown bear can eat 41 kg (90 lb) of food and gain 2–3 kg (4.4–6.6 lb) of fat a day prior to entering its den.[15]

Figure 20: *Captive Asian black bears during an aggressive encounter*

Communication

Bears produce a number of vocal and non-vocal sounds. Tongue-clicking, grunting or chuffing many be made in cordial situations, such as between mothers and cubs or courting couples, while moaning, huffing, sorting or blowing air is made when an individual is stressed. Barking is produced during times of alarm, excitement or to give away the animal's position. Warning sounds include jaw-clicking and lip-popping, while teeth-chatters, bellows, growls, roars and pulsing sounds are made in aggressive encounters. Cubs may squeal, bawl, bleat or scream when in distress and make motor-like humming when comfortable or nursing.[16]

Bears sometimes communicate with visual displays such as standing upright, which exaggerates the individual's size. The chest markings of some species may add to this intimidating display. Staring is an aggressive act and the facial markings of spectacled bears and giant pandas may help draw attention to the eyes during agonistic encounters.[17] Individuals may approach each other by stiff-legged walking with the head lowered. Dominance between bears is asserted by making a frontal orientation, showing the canine teeth, muzzle twisting and neck stretching. A subordinate may respond with a lateral orientation, by turning away and dropping the head and by sitting or lying down.

Figure 21: *Sloth bear rubbing against tree at Nagarhole Tiger Reserve, India*

Bears may mark territory by rubbing against trees and other objects which may serve to spread their scent. This is usually accompanied by clawing and biting the object. Bark may be spread around to draw attention to the marking post.[18] Pandas are known to mark objects with urine and a waxy substance from their anal glands. Polar bears leave behind their scent in their tracks which allow individuals to keep track of one another in the vast Arctic wilderness.

Reproduction and development

The mating system of bears has variously been described as a form of polygyny, promiscuity and serial monogamy. During the breeding season, males take notice of females in their vicinity and females become more tolerant of males. A male bear may visit a female continuously over a period of several days or weeks, depending on the species, to test her reproductive state. During this time period, males try to prevent rivals from interacting with their mate. Courtship may be brief, although in some Asian species, courting pairs may engage in wrestling, hugging, mock fighting and vocalising. Ovulation is induced by mating, which can last up to 30 minutes depending on the species.[19]

Gestation typically lasts 6–9 months, including delayed implantation, and litter size numbers up to four cubs. Giant pandas may give birth to twins but they can only suckle one young and the other is left to die. In northern living species,

Figure 22: *American black bears mating at the North American Bear Center*

Figure 23: *Polar bear mother nursing her cub*

birth takes place during winter dormancy. Cubs are born blind and helpless with at most a thin layer of hair, relying on their mother for warmth. The milk of the female bear is rich in fat and antibodies and cubs may suckle for up to a year after they are born. By 2–3 months, cubs can follow their mother outside the den. They usually follow her on foot, but sloth bear cubs may ride on their mother's back.[20] Male bears play no role in raising young. Infanticide, where an adult male kills the cubs of another, has been recorded in polar bears, brown bears and American black bears but not in other species.[21] Males kill young to bring the female into oestrus. Cubs may flee and the mother defends them even at the cost of her life.

In some species, offspring may become independent around the next spring, through some may stay until the female successfully mates again. Bears reach sexual maturity shortly after they disperse; at around 3–6 years depending on the species. Male Alaskan brown bears and polar bears may continue to grow until they are 11 years old. Lifespan may also vary between species. The brown bear can live an average of 25 years.

Hibernation

Bears of northern regions, including the American black bear and the grizzly bear, hibernate in the winter. During hibernation, the bear's metabolism slows down, its body temperature decreases slightly, and its heart rate slows from a normal value of 55 to just 9 beats per minute. Bears normally do not wake during their hibernation, and can go the entire period without eating, drinking, urinating, or defecating. A fecal plug is formed in the colon, and is expelled when the bear wakes in the spring. If they have stored enough body fat, their muscles remain in good condition, and their protein maintenance requirements are met from recycling waste urea. Female bears give birth during the hibernation period, and are roused when doing so.

Predators, parasites and pathogens

Bears do not have many predators. The most important are humans, and as they started cultivating crops, they increasingly came in conflict with the bears that raided them. Since the invention of firearms, people have been able to kill bears with greater ease. Felids like the tiger may also prey on bears, particularly cubs, which may be also be threatened by canids.

Bears are parasitized by eighty species of parasites, including single-celled protozoans and gastro-intestinal worms, and nematodes and flukes in their heart, liver, lungs and bloodstream. Externally they have ticks, fleas and lice. A study of American black bears found seventeen species of endoparasite including the protozoan *Sarcocystis*, the parasitic worm *Diphyllobothrium mansonoides*,

Figure 24: *Hunters with shot bear, Sweden, early 20th century. This photograph is in the Nordic Museum.*

and the nematodes *Dirofilaria immitis*, *Capillaria aerophila*, *Physaloptera* sp., *Strongyloides* sp. and others. Of these, *D. mansonoides* and adult *C. aerophila* were causing pathological symptoms. By contrast, polar bears have few parasites; many parasitic species need a secondary, usually terrestrial, host, and the polar bear's life style is such that few alternative hosts exist in their environment. The protozoan *Toxoplasma gondii* has been found in polar bears, and the nematode *Trichinella nativa* can cause a serious infection and decline in older polar bears. Bears in North America are sometimes infected by a *Morbillivirus* similar to the canine distemper virus. They are susceptible to infectious canine hepatitis (CAV-1), with free-living black bears dying rapidly of encephalitis and hepatitis.

Relationship with humans

Conservation

In modern times, bears have come under pressure through encroachment on their habitats and illegal trade in bear parts, including the Asian bile bear market, though hunting is now banned, largely replaced by farming. The IUCN lists six bear species as vulnerable; even the two least concern species, the brown bear and the American black bear, are at risk of extirpation in certain areas. In general these two species inhabit remote areas with little interaction with humans, and the main non-natural causes of mortality are hunting, trapping, road-kill and depredation.

Figure 25: *A barrel trap in Grand Teton National Park, Wyoming used to relocate bears away from where they might attack humans*

Laws have been passed in many areas of the world to protect bears from habitat destruction. Public perception of bears is often positive, as people identify with bears due to their omnivorous diets, their ability to stand on two legs, and their symbolic importance. Support for bear protection is widespread, at least in more affluent societies. Where bears raid crops or attack livestock, they may come into conflict with humans. In poorer rural regions, attitudes may be more shaped by the dangers posed by bears, and the economic costs they cause to farmers and ranchers.

Attacks

Several bear species are dangerous to humans, especially in areas where they have become used to people; elsewhere, they generally avoid humans. Injuries caused by bears are rare, but are widely reported. Bears may attack humans in response to being startled, in defense of young or food, or even for predatory reasons.

Figure 26: *The dancing bear by William Frederick Witherington, 1822*

Entertainment, hunting, food and folk medicine

Bears in captivity have for centuries been used for entertainment. They have been trained to dance, and were kept for baiting in Europe at least since the 16th century. There were five bear-baiting gardens in Southwark, London at that time; archaeological remains of three of these have survived. Across Europe, nomadic Romani bear handlers called Ursari lived by busking with their bears from the 12th century.

Bears have been hunted for sport, food, and folk medicine. Their meat is dark and stringy, like a tough cut of beef. In Cantonese cuisine, bear paws are considered a delicacy. Bear meat should be cooked thoroughly, as it can be infected with the parasite *Trichinella spiralis*.

The peoples of eastern Asia use bears' body parts and secretions (notably their gallbladders and bile) as part of traditional Chinese medicine. More than 12,000 bears are thought to be kept on farms in China, Vietnam, and South Korea for the production of bile. Trade in bear products is prohibited under CITES, but bear bile has been detected in shampoos, wine and herbal medicines sold in Canada, the United States and Australia.

Figure 27: *A nomadic ursar, a Romani bear-busker. Drawing by Theodor Aman, 1888*

Literature, art and symbolism

<templatestyles src="Multiple_image/styles.css" />

Onikuma, a Japanese demon bear from *Ehon Hyaku Monogatari*, c. 1841

The Latvian legendary hero Lāčplēsis kills a bear with his bare hands.

There is evidence of prehistoric bear worship, though this is disputed by archaeologists. The prehistoric Finns, Siberian peoples and more recently Koreans considered the bear as the spirit of their forefathers. There is evidence of bear worship in early Chinese and Ainu cultures. In many Native American cultures, the bear is a symbol of rebirth because of its hibernation and re-emergence.[22] The image of the mother bear was prevalent throughout societies in North America and Eurasia, based on the female's devotion and protection of her cubs.[23] Japanese folklore features the Onikuma, a "demon bear" that walks upright. The Ainu of northern Japan, a different people from the Japanese, saw the bear instead as sacred; Hirasawa Byozan painted a scene in documentary style of a bear sacrifice in an Ainu temple, complete with offerings to the dead animal's spirit.

In Korean mythology, a tiger and a bear prayed to Hwanung, the son of the Lord of Heaven, that they might become human. Upon hearing their prayers, Hwanung gave them 20 cloves of garlic and a bundle of mugwort, ordering them to eat only this sacred food and remain out of the sunlight for 100 days. The tiger gave up after about twenty days and left the cave. However, the bear persevered and was transformed into a woman. The bear and the tiger are said to represent two tribes that sought the favor of the heavenly prince.[24] The bear-woman (Ungnyeo; 웅녀/熊女) was grateful and made offerings to Hwanung. However, she lacked a husband, and soon became sad and prayed beneath a "divine birch" tree (Hangul: 신단수; Hanja: 神檀樹 ; RR: *shindansu*) to be blessed with a child. Hwanung, moved by her prayers, took her for his wife and soon she gave birth to a son named Dangun Wanggeom – who was the legendary founder of Gojoseon, the first ever Korean kingdom.

Artio (*Dea Artio* in the Gallo-Roman religion) was a Celtic bear goddess. Evidence of her worship has notably been found at Bern, itself named for the bear. Her name is derived from the Celtic word for "bear", *artos*. In ancient Greece, archaic cult of Artemis in bear form survived into Classical times at Brauron, where young Athenian girls passed an initiation right as *arktai* "she bears".[25] For Artemis and one of her nymphs as a she-bear, see the myth of Callisto.

The constellations of Ursa Major and Ursa Minor, the great and little bears, are named for their supposed resemblance to bears, from the time of Ptolemy.[26]</ref> The nearby star Arcturus means "guardian of the bear", as if it were watching the two constellations. Ursa Major has been associated with a bear for as much as 13,000 years since Paleolithic times, in the widespread Cosmic Hunt myths. These are found on both sides of the Bering land bridge, which was lost to the sea some 11,000 years ago.[27]

Figure 28: *The constellation of Ursa Major as depicted in Urania's Mirror, c. 1825*

Pliny the Elder's *Natural History* (1st century AD) claims that "when first born, [bears] are shapeless masses of white flesh, a little larger than mice; their claws alone being prominent. The mother then licks them gradually into proper shape." This belief was echoed by authors of bestiaries throughout the medieval period.

Bears are mentioned in the Bible; the Second Book of Kings relates the story of the prophet Elisha calling on them to eat the youths who taunted him.[28] Legends of saints taming bears are common in the Alpine zone. In the arms of the bishopric of Freising, the bear is the dangerous totem animal tamed by St. Corbinian and made to carry his civilised baggage over the mountains. Bears similarly feature in the legends of St. Romedius, Saint Gall and Saint Columbanus. This recurrent motif was used by the Church as a symbol of the victory of Christianity over paganism. In the Norse settlements of northern England during the 10th century, a type of "hogback" grave cover of a long narrow block of stone, with a shaped apex like the roof beam of a long house, is carved with a muzzled, thus Christianised, bear clasping each gable end, as in the church at Brompton, North Yorkshire and across the British Isles.

Lāčplēsis, meaning "Bear-slayer", is a Latvian legendary hero who is said to have killed a bear by ripping its jaws apart with his bare hands. However, as revealed in the end of the long epic describing his life, Lāčplēsis' own mother had been a she-bear, and his superhuman strength resided in his bear ears. The

Figure 29: *'The Three Bears'', Arthur Rackham's illustration to English Fairy Tales, by Flora Annie Steel, 1918*

Figure 30: *The Persian Cat, British Lion and Russian Bear in the Anglo-Russian Entente of 1907*

modern Latvian military award Order of Lāčplēsis, called for the hero, is also known as *The Order of the Bear-Slayer*.

Bears are popular in children's stories, including Winnie the Pooh, Paddington Bear, Gentle Ben and "The Brown Bear of Norway". An early version of "Goldilocks and the Three Bears", was published as "The Three Bears" in 1837 by Robert Southey, many times retold, and illustrated in 1918 by Arthur Rackham. The cartoon character Yogi Bear has appeared in numerous comic books, animated television shows and films. The Care Bears began as greeting cards in 1982, and were featured as toys, on clothing and in film. Around the world, many children—and some adults—have teddy bears, stuffed toys in the form of bears, named after the American statesman Theodore Roosevelt when in 1902 he had refused to shoot an American black bear tied to a tree.

Bears, like other animals, may symbolize nations. In 1911, the British satirical magazine *Punch* published a cartoon about the Anglo-Russian Entente by Leonard Raven-Hill in which the British lion watches as the Russian bear sits on the tail of the Persian cat. The Russian Bear has been a common national personification for Russia from the 16th century onwards. Smokey Bear has become a part of American culture since his introduction in 1944, with his message "Only you can prevent forest fires". In the United Kingdom, the bear and staff feature on the heraldic arms of the county of Warwickshire. Bears appear in the canting arms of two cities, Bern and Berlin.

Organizations

The International Association for Bear Research & Management, also known as the International Bear Association, and the Bear Specialist Group of the Species Survival Commission, a part of the International Union for Conservation of Nature focus on the natural history, management, and conservation of bears. Bear Trust International works for wild bears and other wildlife through four core program initiatives, namely Conservation Education, Wild Bear Research, Wild Bear Management, and Habitat Conservation.

Specialty organizations for each of the eight species of bears worldwide include:

- Vital Ground, for the brown bear
- Moon Bears, for the Asiatic black bear
- Black Bear Conservation Coalition, for the North American black bear
- Polar Bears International, for the polar bear
- Bornean Sun Bear Conservation Centre, for the sun bear
- Wildlife SOS, for the sloth bear
- Andean Bear Conservation Project, for the Andean bear
- Chengdu Research Base of Giant Panda Breeding, for the giant panda

Figure 31: *Juvenile pandas at the Chengdu Research Base of Giant Panda Breeding*

References

Bibliography

- Ward, P.; Kynaston, S. (1995). *Wild Bears of the World*. Facts on File, Inc. ISBN 978-0-8160-3245-7.<templatestyles src="Module:Citation/CS1/styles.css"></templatestyles>

Further reading

- Domico, Terry; Newman, Mark (1988). *Bears of the World*. Facts on File, Inc. ISBN 978-0-8160-1536-8.<templatestyles src="Module:Citation/CS1/styles.css"></templatestyles>
- Faulkner, William (1942). *The Bear*[29]. Curley Publishing. ISBN 978-0-7927-0537-6.<templatestyles src="Module:Citation/CS1/styles.css"></templatestyles>
- Brunner, Bernd (2007). *Bears: A Brief History*. Yale University Press. ISBN 978-0-300-12299-2.<templatestyles src="Module:Citation/CS1/styles.css"></templatestyles>

External links

- The Bears Project – Information, reports and images of European brown bears and other living species[30]
- Western Wildlife Outreach – Information on the history, biology, and conservation of North American Grizzly Bears and Black Bears[31]
- The Bear Book and Curriculum Guide – a compilation of stories about all eight species of bears worldwide, including STEM lessons rooted in bear research, ecology, and conservation[32]

Appendix

References

[1] Sweet, Henry (1884) *Anglo-Saxon Reader in Prose and Verse* https://archive.org/details/ anglosaxonreader00sweerich. The Clarendon Press, p. 202.

[2] Ward and Kynaston, pp. 74–77

[3] Treating pinnipeds<ref name="Illiger1811">

[4] Ward and Kynaston, p. 61

[5]

[6] Ward and Kynaston, p.52

[7] Ward and Kynaston, 99

[8] Ward and Kynaston, p. 130

[9]

[10] Ward and Kynaston, pp. 89–92

[11] Ward and Kynaston, p. 87

[12] Ward and Kynaston, p. 89

[13]

[14] Ward and Kynaston, p. 92

[15] Ward and Kynaston, p. 104

[16]

[17]

[18] Ward and Kynaston, p. 122

[19]

[20]

[21] Ward and Kynaston, p. 132

[22] Ward and Kynaston, p. 17

[23] Ward and Kynaston, pp. 12–13

[24] http://www.san-shin.org/Dan-gun_Myth.html

[25] Burkert, Walter, *Greek Religion*, 1985:263.

[26] Ptolemy named the constellations in Greek, Ἄρκτος μεγάλη (Arktos Megale) and Ἄρκτος μικρά (Arktos Mikra), the great and little bears.<ref name="Ridpath">

[27] reviewed at

[28] Second Book of Kings, 2:23–25

[29] https://docs.google.com/viewer?a=v&pid=sites&srcid= ZGVmYXVsdGRvbWFpbnx0aGV2aXJ0dWFsZW5nbGlzaG5vdGVib29rfGd4OjFiYjYyNDA4NTQwZC

[30] http://www.medvede.sk/index1.php

[31] http://www.bearinfo.org/

[32] http://beartrust.org/the-bear-book-and-curriculum-guide-to-the-bear-book

Article Sources and Contributors

The sources listed for each article provide more detailed licensing information including the copyright status, the copyright owner, and the license conditions.

Bear *Source:* https://en.wikipedia.org/w/index.php?oldid=865593135 *License:* Creative Commons Attribution-Share Alike 3.0 *Contributors:* 4444hhhh, 564dude, Accuruss, Anaxial, Anomalocaris, Arjayay, Asarelah, BD2412, Biruitorul, Blanche of King's Lynn, Bobnorwal, Chiswick Chap, Chumash11, Colonies Chris, Cwmhiraeth, DrChrissy, Dunkleosteus77, Fish and karate, Gilo1969, Gronk Oz, Hanif Al Husaini, Harsimaja, Headbomb, Jarble, Leo1pard, LittleJerry, Mandruss, Mariomassone, Mr Stephen, Nick Number, Nikkimaria, Northamerica1000, Offbeat91, Plantdrew, Pretended leer, Rjwilmsi, Rtkat3, SchreiberBike, Smasongarrison, The Rambling Man, TheFrenchTickler1031, Tom.Reding, Ubcule, Wbm1058, Wetman, WolfmanSF 1

Image Sources, Licenses and Contributors

The sources listed for each image provide more detailed licensing information including the copyright status, the copyright owner, and the license conditions.

Image *Source:* https://en.wikipedia.org/w/index.php?title=File:Padlock-silver.svg *Contributors:* AzaToth, BotMultichill, BotMultichillT, Gurch, Jarekt, Kallerna, Multichill, Perhelion, Rd232, Riana, Sarang, Siebrand, Steinsplitter, 4 anonymous edits 1

Image *Source:* https://en.wikipedia.org/w/index.php?title=File:Symbol_support_vote.svg *License:* Public Domain *Contributors:* Anomie, Fastily, Jo-Jo Eumerus 1

Image *Source:* https://en.wikipedia.org/w/index.php?title=File:2010-brown-bear.jpg *License:* Creative Commons Attribution-Sharealike 3.0 *Contributors:* User:Yathin sk 1

Image *Source:* https://en.wikipedia.org/w/index.php?title=File:Red_Pencil_Icon.png *License:* Creative Commons Zero *Contributors:* User:Peter coxhead 1

Image *Source:* https://en.wikipedia.org/w/index.php?title=File:Dagger-14-plain.png *License:* Creative Commons Zero *Contributors:* RexxS 1

Figure 1 *Source:* https://en.wikipedia.org/w/index.php?title=File:Plithocyon_armagnacensis.JPG *License:* Public Domain *Contributors:* Ghedo 4

Figure 2 *Source:* https://en.wikipedia.org/w/index.php?title=File:Teufelshöhle-Höhlenbär-Dreiviertelprofil.jpg *License:* Creative Commons Attribution-Sharealike 3.0 *Contributors:* Ra'ike (see also: de:Benutzer:Ra'ike) 5

Image *Source:* https://en.wikipedia.org/w/index.php?title=File:Lydekker_-_Ocelot_(white_background).JPG *License:* Public Domain *Contributors:* Wyman & Sons Limited 6

Image *Source:* https://en.wikipedia.org/w/index.php?title=File:Dogs,_jackals,_wolves,_and_foxes_(Plate_XI).jpg *License:* Public Domain *Contributors:* Mariomassone, William Harris 6

Image *Source:* https://en.wikipedia.org/w/index.php?title=File:Hemicyon_white_background.jpg *License:* Public Domain *Contributors:* Mariomassone 6

Image *Source:* https//en.wikipedia.org *License:* Public Domain *Contributors:* Iconographia Zoologica 6

Image *Source:* https://en.wikipedia.org/w/index.php?title=File:Faroe_stamp_227_grey_seal_(Phoca_vitulina)_white_background.jpg *License:* Faroe stamps *Contributors:* Bárður Jákupsson 6

Image *Source:* https//en.wikipedia.org *License:* Public Domain *Contributors:* Mariomassone, Ruff tuff cream puff 6

Image *Source:* https://en.wikipedia.org/w/index.php?title=File:Mustela_eversmanii_(white_background).png *Contributors:* User:Петроченко Віктор Іванович 6

Image *Source:* https://en.wikipedia.org/w/index.php?title=File:Kolponomos_newportensis_.jpg *Contributors:* User:A. C. Tatarinov 7

Image *Source:* https://en.wikipedia.org/w/index.php?title=File:Recherches_pour_servir_à_l'histoire_naturelle_des_mammifères_(Pl._50)_(white_background).jpg *License:* Public Domain *Contributors:* Iconographia Zoologica 7

Image *Source:* https://en.wikipedia.org/w/index.php?title=File:Spectacled_bear_(1829).jpg *License:* Public Domain *Contributors:* G. Cuvier 7

Image *Source:* https://en.wikipedia.org/w/index.php?title=File:Daphoenodon_superbus_by_R._B._Horsfall_(coloured).png *License:* Public Domain *Contributors:* Robert Bruce Horsfall 8

Image *Source:* https://en.wikipedia.org/w/index.php?title=File:Cambridge_Natural_History_Mammalia_Fig_230_white_background.jpg *License:* Public Domain *Contributors:* Mariomassone 8

Image *Source:* https//en.wikipedia.org *License:* Public Domain *Contributors:* Iconographia Zoologica 9

Image *Source:* https//en.wikipedia.org *License:* Public Domain *Contributors:* A ri gi bod, MPF, Mariomassone 9

Image *Source:* https//en.wikipedia.org *License:* Public Domain *Contributors:* Iconographia Zoologica 9

Image *Source:* https//en.wikipedia.org *License:* Public Domain *Contributors:* Iconographia Zoologica 9

Image *Source:* https://en.wikipedia.org/w/index.php?title=File:Tremarctos_ornatus_1824_(flipped).jpg *License:* Public Domain *Contributors:* Iconographia Zoologica 9

Figure 3 *Source:* https://en.wikipedia.org/w/index.php?title=File:Kolponomos_newportensis_.jpg *Contributors:* User:A. C. Tatarinov 10

Figure 4 *Source:* https://en.wikipedia.org/w/index.php?title=File:Hemicyon.jpg *License:* Public Domain *Contributors:* FunkMonk, Ixtzib, Kilom691, Ltshears, Materialscientist, OgreBot 2, Ubcule 10

Figure 5 *Source:* https://en.wikipedia.org/w/index.php?title=File:Agriotherium_maraghanus_mandible.JPG *License:* Creative Commons Attribution-Sharealike 3.0 *Contributors:* User:Ghedoghedo 11

Figure 6 *Source:* https://en.wikipedia.org/w/index.php?title=File:Indarctos_atticus.jpg *Contributors:* User:Ghedoghedo 11

Figure 7 *Source:* https://en.wikipedia.org/w/index.php?title=File:Bai_yun_giant_panda.jpg *License:* GNU Free Documentation License *Contributors:* Mfield, Matthew Field, http://www.photography.mattfield.com 12

Figure 8 *Source:* https://en.wikipedia.org/w/index.php?title=File:Arctotherium.jpg *License:* Public Domain *Contributors:* Clpo13, FunkMonk, Innotata, Kersti Nebelsiek, Maky, WolfmanSF 12

Figure 9 *Source:* https://en.wikipedia.org/w/index.php?title=File:Bear_sitting.JPG *License:* Creative Commons Attribution-Sharealike 3.0 *Contributors:* User:Bhaskaranaidu 13

Figure 10 *Source:* https://en.wikipedia.org/w/index.php?title=File:Ice_Age_Cave_Bear_Skeleton.jpg *Contributors:* User:Rauantiques 13

Figure 11 *Source:* https://en.wikipedia.org/w/index.php?title=File:AlaskanBear_closeup.jpg *License:* Creative Commons Attribution 2.0 *Contributors:* FlickreviewR, Rocket000 14

Image *Source:* https://en.wikipedia.org/w/index.php?title=File:Polar_Bear_AdF.jpg *Contributors:* User:Arturo de Frias Marques 18

Image *Source:* https://en.wikipedia.org/w/index.php?title=File:Sepilok_Sabah_BSBCC-photos-by-Wong-Siew-Te-06.jpg *License:* Creative Commons Attribution-Sharealike 3.0 Germany *Contributors:* Cccefalon, Natuur12 19

Figure 12 *Source:* https://en.wikipedia.org/w/index.php?title=File:Bear_foot.jpg *License:* Public Domain *Contributors:* Richard Owen 19

Figure 13 *Source:* https://en.wikipedia.org/w/index.php?title=File:Black_bear_large.jpg *License:* Public Domain *Contributors:* Mike Bender/U.S. Fish and Wildlife Service 20

Figure 14 *Source:* https://en.wikipedia.org/w/index.php?title=File:Ursus_arctos_01_MWNH_145_(cropped).JPG *License:* Creative Commons Attribution-Sharealike 3.0 *Contributors:* Klaus Rassinger und Gerhard Cammerer, Museum Wiesbaden 21

Figure 15 *Source:* https://en.wikipedia.org/w/index.php?title=File:Spectacled_Bear_161_(2).jpg *License:* Creative Commons Attribution-Sharealike 3.0 *Contributors:* User:Futureman1199 23

Figure 16 *Source:* https://en.wikipedia.org/w/index.php?title=File:Bear_tracks_(5062843250).jpg *License:* Creative Commons Attribution 2.0 *Contributors:* Superior National Forest 24

Figure 17 *Source:* https://en.wikipedia.org/w/index.php?title=File:Giant_Panda_Tai_Shan.JPG *License:* Creative Commons Attribution-Sharealike 2.5 *Contributors:* Fernando Revilla 24

Figure 18 *Source:* https://en.wikipedia.org/w/index.php?title=File:Bear_Alaska_(3).jpg *License:* Creative Commons Attribution 2.0 *Contributors:* Carl Chapman from Phoenix, usa 25

Figure 19 *Source:* https://en.wikipedia.org/w/index.php?title=File:Polar_bear_(Ursus_maritimus)_with_its_prey.jpg *Contributors:* User:AWeith 26

Figure 20 *Source:* https://en.wikipedia.org/w/index.php?title=File:Ursus_thibetanus_01.JPG *License:* Creative Commons Attribution-Sharealike 3.0 *Contributors:* H. Zell 27

Figure 21 *Source:* https://en.wikipedia.org/w/index.php?title=File:Standing_Sloth_Bear.jpg *Contributors:* User:Chengappabb 28

Figure 22 *Source:* https://en.wikipedia.org/w/index.php?title=File:Black_Bears_mating.jpg *License:* Creative Commons Attribution 3.0 *Contributors:* North American Bear Center 29

Figure 23 *Source:* https://en.wikipedia.org/w/index.php?title=File:Cub_polar_bear_is_nursing_2.OGG *Contributors:* - 29

Figure 24 *Source:* https://en.wikipedia.org/w/index.php?title=File:Björnjakt_i_Dalarna_-_Nordiska_Museet_-_NMA.0052736.jpg *License:* Public Domain *Contributors:* Achird, Zejo, Ö 31

Figure 25 *Source:* https://en.wikipedia.org/w/index.php?title=File:Bear_trap_GTNP1.jpg *License:* Creative Commons Attribution-Sharealike 3.0 *Contributors:* Acroterion 32

Figure 26 *Source:* https://en.wikipedia.org/w/index.php?title=File:The_dancing_bear_by_William_Frederick_Witherington.jpg *License:* Public Domain *Contributors:* Chiswick Chap, Electron, Warburg, Лобачев Владимир 33

Figure 27 *Source:* https://en.wikipedia.org/w/index.php?title=File:Theodor_Aman_-_Ursarul.jpg *License:* Public Domain *Contributors:* Bogdan, Chiswick Chap, Dahn, Error, Fabartus, Flominator, MGA73, Mattes, Mvelam, Okki, Skrod, Warburg, Лобачев Владимир, 1 anonymous edits 34

Image *Source:* https://en.wikipedia.org/w/index.php?title=File:ShunsenOniguma.jpg *License:* Public Domain *Contributors:* Takehara Shunsen (竹原春泉) 34

Image *Source:* https://en.wikipedia.org/w/index.php?title=File:Brīvības_piemineklis-Lāčplēsis.png *License:* Creative Commons Attribution 3.0 *Contributors:* Peters J. Vecrumba 34

44

License

Index

9789352979820